Saying I miss you never felt like enough

Kai Giannelli

BookLeaf Publishing

Presentation by *BookLeaf Publishing*

Web: www.bookleafpub.com

E-mail: info@bookleafpub.com

ISBN: 9789358735635

First edition 2023

To all the ones I've lost and all the ones I've found, you've all my heart just the same.

Who meets you at the gates
when you've spent your
whole life fighting them?

I met a boy once,
he asked me why I'd come.
I told him I hadn't meant to,
I'd gotten lost in the space between.

He asked me why I'd come,
with my lips pulled tight I whispered —
I'd gotten lost in the space between
a reason and a promise.

With my lips pulled tight I whispered —
I fell for who felt like heaven.
A reason and a promise,
all I needed to say was goodbye.

I fell for who felt like heaven,
I told him I hadn't meant to,
all I needed to say was goodbye…
I met a boy once.

A day of missing you

12am
I fall asleep wrapped in your old blanket
4am
I wake with wet cheeks from a dream of you
laughing
8am
I look at the ceiling and wave I say good
morning
9am
I hear you walking in the kitchen I hold the
counter and count to 100
10am
I can still hear you I wonder if it will ever be
quiet
2pm
I sit in your favorite chair and tell you about my
day I ask you how yours was but I didn't hear
your answer
3pm
I'm sorry
4pm
I put two plates out in case you were hungry
5pm
I've picked up drinking again I'm sorry
7pm

Do you think of me Do you see me alone and
feel sorry for me
9pm
I miss you I feel you around me You're
everywhere Everything
12am
I fall asleep wrapped in your old blanket it
doesn't smell like you anymore

I'm sorry

Subtle

Perhaps the most subtle pain
is that of a heart which cracks
then shatters all at once

When all else fails I'll remember you, I'll be by your side, and I'll carry you over

The smell of antiseptic
digs its claws into skin.

The fluorescent lights
burn circles into my eyes.

I float through the hall
of disembodied moans and forgotten faces
with a nauseating thought -
You're here and you're scared.

I hurry past the starved doors
begging for visitors

Until my feet stall at yours

I can't bring myself to knock
I slide in like a wisp of smoke
unsure and unnerving

You're in a bed
you look so small so tired.

A sound squeaks out
of my throat
and I tell myself

I can't cry in front of you.

Your hand shakes when you see me
your voice cracks and
you start to cry

You tell me you love me
and you ask if I'll come again

If I'll bring you home to your son

And my heart shatters
the pieces tear me apart

My tears burn as they fall
as I tell you

Of course I'll bring you home
and when you fall asleep
your hand slips from mine.

I whisper the only prayer I know
onto your cold skin
I love you always.

When you lose yourself in the fog I'll be the light to guide you through

I'll remember your smile
when you're surprised.

I'll remember the color of your eyes
when you're laughing.

I'll remember how it felt
to hug you when our hearts ached.

I'll remember your laugh
and how you'd joke.

I'll remember the way
you loved me.

I'll remember how
you held my hand.

I'll remember how
you watched me grow.

I'll remember how

we'd laugh.

I'll remember you
when you've forgotten.

On a rainy night under the guise of a reaper we'll meet once more

The home you first loved me in
sits stagnat
I hear they tore it down.

The shop you first held me in
fell through the cracks
I saw the cobwebs take it.

The day you told me I care
strangles me
I wonder if you knew I cared too.

The thought of you alone
beneath me
confused.

The thought that you were scared
makes those words
fish hooks in my throat.

How do I tell you I care about you
I love you

and I'm so sorry

When I've no idea
where your head rests?

How do I tell you I miss you
when I lost you
so long ago?

The thought that your soul
your spirit
might not recognize me now—

Keeps me awake with sorrow.

If no one is there to pick up the call can you say that you called at all?

On the snowy night that
Death calls for me
may I ask that he leave a message?

Would he listen to who
had called upon him
who wished for his hand
and decided —

Not yet

Would he hear my cries
of human desire
of sorrow when I say

I can't leave
I've not yet left my mark

What is in my eyes when I'm watching you be returned to the Earth?

If I held your hand would you still be nervous?
If I went with you would you still cry?

When the dirt comes to meet you,
and you're tumbling down,
and the dark comes rushing in,
are you crying?

Is it what you imagined it would be?

When you can't say what hurts and you can't remember your name I'll be

Beneath the clouds shrouded by rain
I can be whoever you need
to ease the pain.

Behind the words that you read
I can be the story
that pulls you into sleep

In the sea of memories can you find your way back to the shore?

Your eyes are choppy waters
the pupil a ghost ship
with set sails to nowhere
wondering where everyone's gone

The pupil a ghost ship
watching all the others pass by
wondering where everyone's gone
forgetting why you started sailing in the first
place

Watching all the others pass by
a fading thought rolls on the waves
wondering where everyone's gone
where will you go from here?

A fading thought rolls on the waves
with set sails to nowhere
where will you go from here
Your eyes are choppy waters

I'd open my chest and pull
out the girl you thought I was
if it meant I could save you

If you would so need me to
I'd be the version of me
that you remember.

If it would ease your creaking bones
I could be your granddaughter
who had your crooked smile.

If it could give you peace
I would claw her out of
the pit of my soul.

I'd wear her as the mask
she always was
to give you one more performance.

To give you one last thing
you can remember.

What once killed you is what now consumes me

With the eyes of my father
it's no wonder that
my mother
stays clear.

With the eyes of my father
I see the tones of him
in the way the earth
feels heavy on me.

With the eyes of my father
I feel the weight
of his demons
climbing onto me.

With the eyes of my father
I know the pain
the fear
that consumes him.

With the eyes of my father
I see guilt for what it is
a manifestation of
all I wished I could be.

With the eyes of my father
I know I am made
in his image
and I am broken
just the same.

I still call your phone just to hear you tell me you can't pick up

Today I sat where we met last.
I ran my fingers along the spine of the chair
hoping to feel that it was still a space
I could call mine.

Today I walked by your house.
the air smelt of coffee and lavender,
the air circled round me with arms so gentle
that I called your name.

Today I looked at the sky.
as blue as your favorite jacket,
and I wondered if you remembered
how we used to laugh.

Today I thought of you when it rained.
I looked for you out my window
and prayed that I'd see you if only to say

I'm sorry I wasn't there then
but I'm here now and
here I'll stay.

If I said I'd never forget you
and now I can't recall how
your voices does that make
me a liar?

Some nights I find
I can't recall the
Sound of your voice.

Some nights my eyes
Only find smoke
When I think of you.

Some nights I drink
Myself into stillness
To deny what's happened.

To deny that I broke
My promise to you.

On that night I wonder if you heard me screaming or if you were already gone

The wind beckons me forward
with the promise of a
twisted tale.

I follow like a sheep to a shepherd
my legs fold underneath me
and I listen.

I listen as the wind screeches
as it whips around me
reaching a crescendo.

I listen as the wind whispers
in a tone so sorrowful
it rips my heart apart —

death has knocked
death has called
and death's calls
they're being answered.

A sound comes

from an animal
or me?

I could not tell.

My body quivers
my heart implodes
my eyes flood.

For there are no words
there are no reactions
that suffice when —

The reaper has reaped what he's sowed.

May you find your way to a life you always dreamed of

Tonight when flames cover you
I hope it reminds you
of our first embrace.

I hope it reminds you of
the times we cooked
and the times we sat by the fire.

I hope it reminds you of
how love covered you
everyday.

Tonight when flames cover you
and time ceases
I hope you remember

I'm by your side.

Would you believe me if I got on my knees and told you I regret everything?

We'll meet again
in a crowded coffee shop
in line for our groceries
or at a funeral

Our eyes will connect
in between them
sorrow, regret
anger, embarrassment
hatred, longing.

My voice will carry to you
it will miss your ears
but perhaps land on your shoulders

Are you happy? It will come out choked
your eyes will leave mine
looking towards the floor
and when you look back to me

I see all the years we spent
and all the years we threw away

Your voice will carry to me
it will miss my ears
and pierce my heart

You do not get to ask me that.

The darkened sky above a rooftop always reminded me of you

Could my story
be so tragic
that someone
would —
cry for me?

Could my story
be so tragic
that the l'appel du vide
would —
remind them of me?

Could my story
be so tragic
that centuries from now
lovers and loners would —
claim me as theirs?

The child, the husband, the fight, the betrayal

My back sticks to the wall
the heat rises to my face
and you lean down to ask me
if I want you at all.

If I'll dance for you
if I'll kiss you
I slide down the wall.

My father sees you out
your hands on your wife's back
you look back and blow
a kiss.

My father is laughing
I remember the sound
of clinking bottles.

You pulled me by my waist
onto your lap
and told me I'm built like my mother.

I ask to be let go
your fingers dig deeper

my thighs start to burn.

My father is laughing
my mother is with your wife
your lips are on my neck

Your son has his hands on my thighs
you tell me I'll belong to you both
and when I finally get away

My father yells at me for ruining the mood
and when I hear his voice
and I see your smile and dripping lips

A piece of me shriveled and died
with the knowledge of all
that I lost.

Had you'd loved me at all
you'd have realized how far I
would fall

If you had loved me at all
you would have held me together

If you had loved me at all
you wouldn't have been the one

To cut me down at the knees
and laugh at my fall.

The mourning never ends the sun just sets

When I am no longer a presence
may my soul be laid to rest
and all that I held be burned.

When my life becomes a memory
let it be remembered that there were
many whom I'd had not the chance to love.

When you mourn me
mourn not only myself,
grieve for the ones who were first.

Mourn the ones who fell
who were shunned
who were exiled.

Before you mourn me,
before my soul becomes distant,
know that this is a cyclical life.

Just as those before me laid to rest
the ones after me will find their way
to the earth's warm dirt.

And to you, who may find it concerning
these lives are lost, thrown out, cut
these lives were not meant to end yet.

And to you, who may find these words
I send you off with a wave of strength
I shall protect you with my spirit.

And to you who may mourn before they
feel that they're allowed to be born
you've always had the right to live.

And to you, who will surely hunt us
who will smell our existence like a hound
I wish you nothing.